INTERNET SUCCESS KEY

KEY

How I suffered and how I conquered

Complete guide to making profit on the internet business program

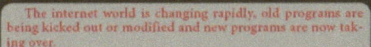

Written By;
Yekini Monsuru Abisoye
Skype: yatuem.oxygen
www.facebook.com/yekini.monsuru
http://y2mread.com:

TABLE OF CONTENTS

1. INTRODUCTION

The internet world is changing rapidly, old programs are being kicked out or modified and new programs are now taking over. The problem with Internet experts and online marketer is that they keep on doing or using the methods of about 6 years old and they expect it to be giving them the same result, that's impossible.

I have suffered a lot in the online world, many fake and bad programs has made me to lose hope in internet business sometimes ago, I invested in many programs and at the end of the day, they swallowed my money, but today I am happy to be an internet marketer because I have recovered times twenty of the money I lost, and I am ready to share my success blue print with you; also I will tell you some of the programs that has swallowed my investment in order for you to avoid those programs, they are not going area.

I have suffered from these fake programs and today, I have conquered.

In this book, I am going to show you how you can start profiting on the internet easily and profitably, I will show the new system that works.

Many E-books will teach you only one program and that's all, they do not always consider whether you have enough capital to start the program or not, I have read many E-books and at the end of the day I cannot put what I read into practice because of the high startup capital. But for me, I realize that all fingers are not equal, what can be easy as pie for one might not be comfortable for another.

So, in this book, I will teach you two new working programs that you will be making money from. The first one is a free set up program and the second program requires little investment. I will shed more light on this soon.

I hope you will enjoy the book and if you want to chat with me on Face-book, here is the link below.

www.facebook.com/yekini.monsuru
Yekini Monsuru Abisoye
Skype: yatuem.oxygen
Admin@y2mread.com
yekinimonsuru@zukul.com
Internet marketer

2. HOW IT ALL STARTED

How it all started, online world, money making program, the work flow, the money flow and your share of the success.

Well, leave all the crap above, I know many will be interested in how to make money online and they are not really interested about the origin of the money making program.

It is really good to know the origin of internet program, their work flow, how money circulates within their members and their authenticity. There are many programs on the internet and don't tell me you want to invest in a program without knowing how it works.

Like I said earlier, I will be showing on how to run two programs and If you like, you can run a single one, there is no crime in it except that the more program you runs the bigger your profit is. The first program is a revenue sharing program which involve sharing money within members, this type of program is an old program indeed and the old school method is that you must look for certain numbers of people before you can earn from it and if you cannot get these people, what happened; you get nothing out of the program, OMG that hurts and sucks. Internet researchers modify this obsolete revenue sharing program into a paying program so that if you cannot bring people in, your money can work for you.

The second program is an entirely new program which has become viral in today's marketing and profit making. Imagine if all the work is being done for you and what you have to is to sit, relax and earn money. This program is for both marketers and profit makers; it is equipped with unbelievable tools in which no one has ever thought of before.

In the next chapter, I will show you the dangers of internet business, so that you will avoid jumping on unnecessary programs.

3. THE GOOD GUYS; THE BAD GUYS

Who are the good guys and who are the bad guys? This look confusing to you as I can read your mind right now, so will you please give me a chance to explain it to you?

Allow me to use a physical world to explain, let us assume that you want to buy food stuff from a particular physical market place where there are many sellers, you do not know these sellers before but you want to buy from just one. You will agree with me that if you are not careful, you might end up buying counterfeit food stuff because not every seller in the market will be good. In fact, 80% of the sellers might be bad sellers and just 20% might be good.

So how will you know the bad sellers from the good sellers? How are you going to know that you will not end up buying bad food stuff from a bad seller? It is simple and easy.

1. You need a mentor; someone who has bought from the seller before
2. You need a well known secure seller to buy from
3. You need a recommendation from people
4. You need proof and result

The online world work in such manner, there are many bad programs online destroying the reputation of the good ones, many people wants to invest online but they are scared of being duped at the end of the day.

I have tested and joined many programs as an internet researcher and out of let us say 20 programs, only 3-5 are real.

Here are the lists of programs I have tested and they swallowed my money till today. I have proof of my account profile with them. Do not ever invest in any High yield investment program, they are 99.9% fraudulent. The remaining 0.1% means I do not want to zero up my mind on them. There are some revenue sharing programs that are also not real. So readers, I advise you to look before you leap.

FAKE AND DUBIOUS PROGRAMS

- Bit-invest.com
- Reality-networkers.com
- Ptcbank.net
- All HYIP programs
- Pyripo.com
- Chokobanks.com
- Autoprofit.com
- Nanoparks.com

And many more.........

All these programs above swallowed my money. So be careful.

Although I have profited with many programs as well and I am making cool money from them, but in this book, I will give you just two as I promised.

1. Paying ads program
2. Guaranteed sign up program

If you need more programs or any question, kindly contact me through my Face book and email.
www.facebook.com/yekini.monsuru
admin@y2mread.com

Let's roll to the next chapter…….
Are you ready?

4. REGISTRATION WITH PAYMENT PROCESSORS

The first step to take is to register with payment processors and if you already have them, congratulations and shake hand with me right now.

It is very important to set up your payment processors, it is a pivot in which money flow in and out of your program; oh I can see that you are ready to read it well now. Well it is not something serious; it is just a simple few steps.

You have to register with one payment processor if you are from US, UK, and Australia but if you are from African countries and some part of Asia, you will need two.

FIRST PAYMENT PROCESSOR

You need a PayPal account, it is very simple to set up, walk up now to http://www.paypal.com and click on sign up. Fill out the registration form, go to your email and confirmed your account, add your mobile number at the profile settings area and confirm it, that's all, you are live on PayPal. The next step is to connect you credit/debit card to PayPal, and you can also connect you' your bank account. PayPal will even guide you on the set up process.

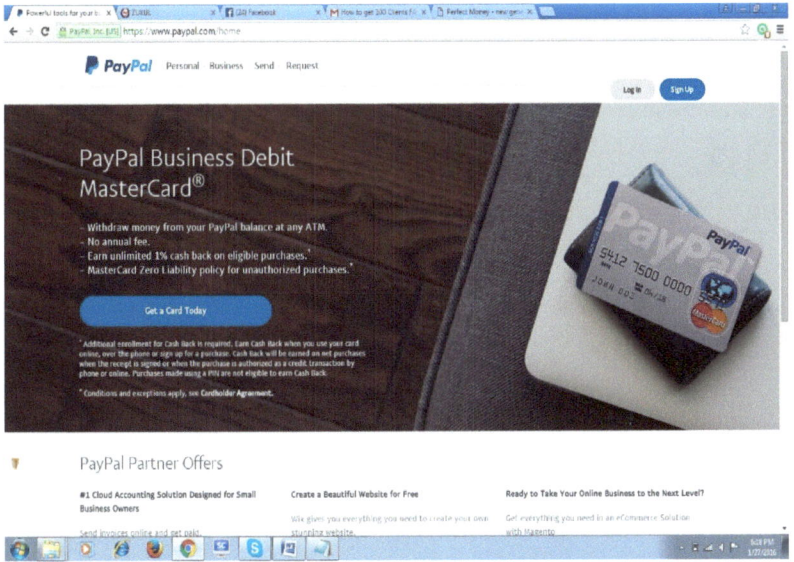

If you already have a US, UK and Australia PayPal, move on now to the next chapter because you can send out money from your PayPal account and as well receive money with it.

If you are from African countries, and some part of Asia and you have already registered with PayPal, move on to the next payment processor. The reason is that you can only use your PayPal to send out money but you cannot receive with it, so you need another payment processor to receive money from your program.

Simple as pie I guess, or is it difficult? I believe it's not.

SECOND PAYMENT PROCESSOR

Go to **www.perfectmoney.is** and register there as a personal account, confirm your account in your email, take note of your account ID, go to the settings section to verify your account, although the verification is not compulsory you must do it immediately, you can get along with next chapter.

Understood?

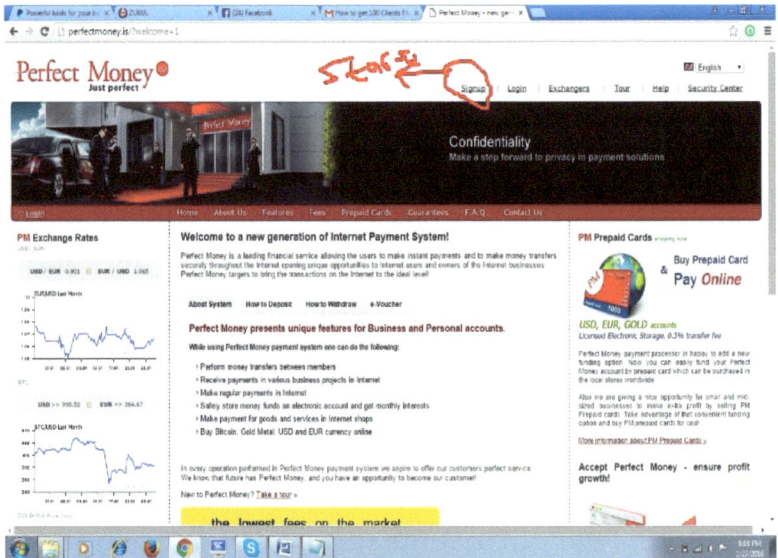

If you need have any question as regard the set up, connect with me on Face book.

www.facebook.com/yekini.monsuru
admin@y2mread.com

5. REGISTRATION WITH A TRUSTED AND PAYING PROGRAM

Now you are getting closer to success, let me inform you that you can be making $200 to $700 per day with this mind blowing program I am about to introduce to you. Surprised? And I can see you are about to ask how? Or you feel like saying this is impossible. Well every impossible mission is always made possible by Tom Cruise; do you remember that Actor? Of course you do.

Back to business, now you have to click the link below to get started, everybody goes through the process and you will not be the first person to do this, I did it also.

CLICK HERE

Or you can press ctrl and click the image above to start your registration

You will be taken to a page where you have to input your name and email address and finally you will find yourself in the program landing page. You are going to do these just ones. Now click on Join us or sign up to join the program, after registration, you will be taken to a page where you will see your metadata, but that is not necessary now.

Go to your email and confirm your sign up and after that you are good to go.

Login to your account, click on your profile settings and add your payment processor, if you can receive money with PayPal add it but if you cannot, you have to add your perfect money account ID.

That's all for registration...

Sit tight now, because you are going to get your pant wet in the next chapter.

6. YOUR SUCCES KEY

Okay, it is high time you start making profit; you have been waiting for this since the beginning of this book. Are you ready to take the key from me now; I know you must be ready for it by now.

Log in to your account now, and the next page you will see is your profile data immediately after you log in. look down at the ad pack/shares section and you will see that you have zero ad pack on your list. Remember I am not even talking about you doing certain job now; we want to put your money into work now.

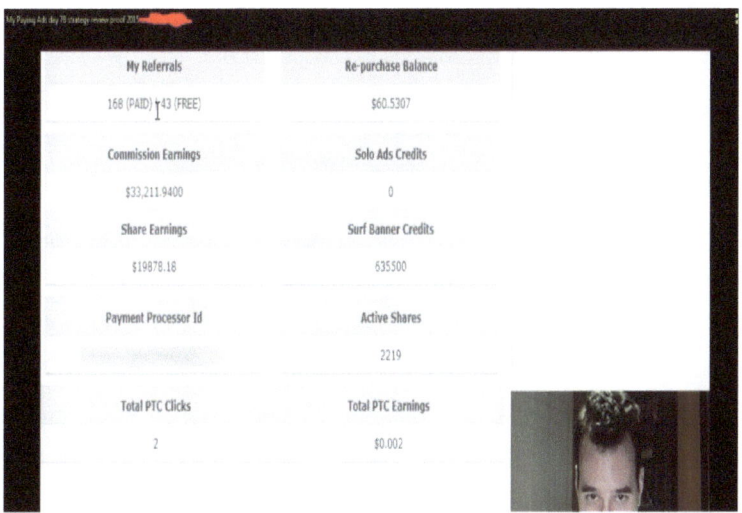

What you are going to do now is to go to the finance tab at the upper tab of the page and ADD FUND into your account with your PayPal account, the minimum of fund you can add into your account is $5, I recommend you to add like $50 if you have it for faster result.

Now you have money in your account, what's next? Forward match to buy ADPACK tab, and buy $5 pack each in 10 places within a day separately, you will have return profit on every ADPACK you purchase every day, that's sweet UHHHHH.

Now on that your $50 you invest, you will be having minimum of $75 return...

That's small right?

RELAX>>>>

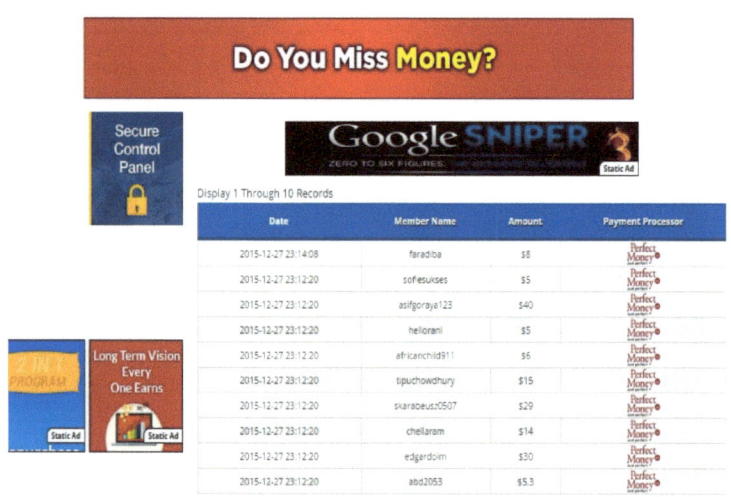

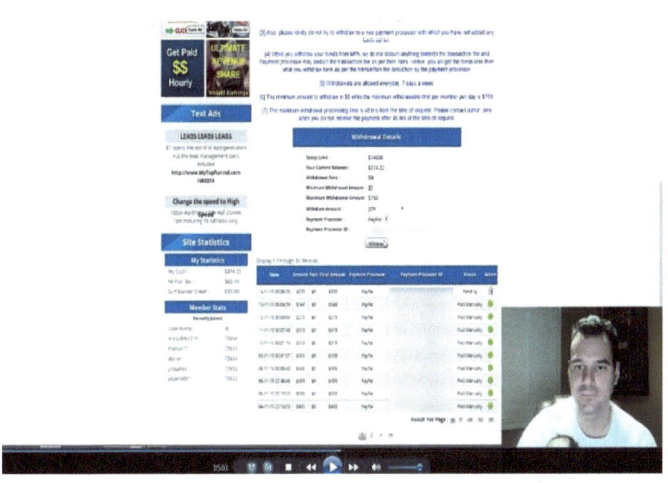

You Can Make Only 1 Withdrawal Requests Per Day.

Display 1 Through 12 Records

Date	Amount	Fees	Final Amount	Payment Processor		Status	Action
15-11-15 00:04:46	$374	$0	$374	PayPal		Pending	
14-11-15 00:06:35	$338	$0	$338	PayPal		Pending	
13-11-15 00:04:39	$348	$0	$348	PayPal		Paid Manually	
12-11-15 00:00:50	$273	$0	$273	PayPal		Paid Manually	
11-11-15 00:07:48	$319	$0	$319	PayPal		Paid Manually	
10-11-15 00:01:10	$319	$0	$319	PayPal		Paid Manually	
09-11-15 00:01:57	$309	$0	$309	PayPal		Paid Manually	
08-11-15 00:05:43	$405	$0	$405	PayPal		Paid Manually	
06-11-15 22:46:49	$450	$0	$450	PayPal			

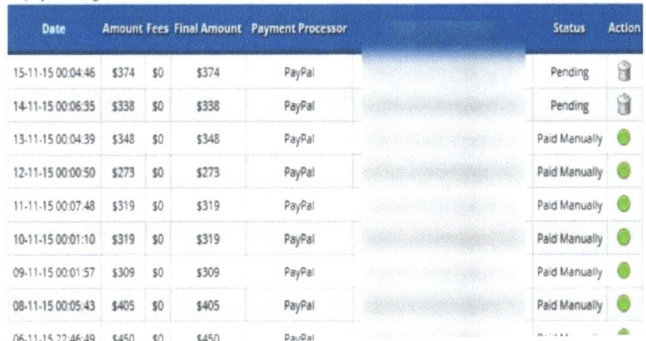

Now you have $75 in your account the next day, go ahead and buy another $10 ADPACK in 7 places the next day with your $75 and you will end up with $110 the next day; it seems we are doubling up, right?

Now with your $110, purchase another pack of $10 each with all your money within a day and next you will have $180, and on, and on, and on for one good month.

At the end of the month, your account will be showing nothing less than $500.

That sound sweet right?

Now start purchasing $50 each ad pack and you will receive the shock of your life

Another interesting thing is that the ad pack you were buying, you will be receiving banner credits every time you buy and you can be using your banner credit to advertise other programs like the one I am going to introduce to you in the next chapter.

7.   GET ZUKULED

Do you remember how Jesus Christ baptized people with holy water? Go down on your kneels now because you about to be baptized.

Oh sorry allow me to say you are about to be ZUKULED.

This program works like a magic and you will not believe it if I tell you that the experts do the work and you earn the money, surprise, UHN?

You better don't be because it is what people has been earning money from early this year and it is so sad you have not heard about it.

Okay, time to get serious, let's leave all those craps. Are you ready to be zukuled?

Now get started by clicking the link below and you will be taken to a page where you have to fill out your name and email address and then onto the zukul homepage where you will sign up.

Press CTRL and click on the link below

CLICK HERE TO START

Let me remind you that you need $99 to get on board with this program and once you are in, Experts will bring your signed up to you like a piece of cake.

The payment is divided into two parts; the first $50 payment is for zukul membership while the second $49 payment is for your sign up. After you have joined the Zukul family, all you need is to sit, relax and wait for your sign up like a Groom waiting for her Bride.

They might just ask you for your 2% activity by liking their post and sharing it on Face book and that's all, nothing more. Or is it too good to be true?

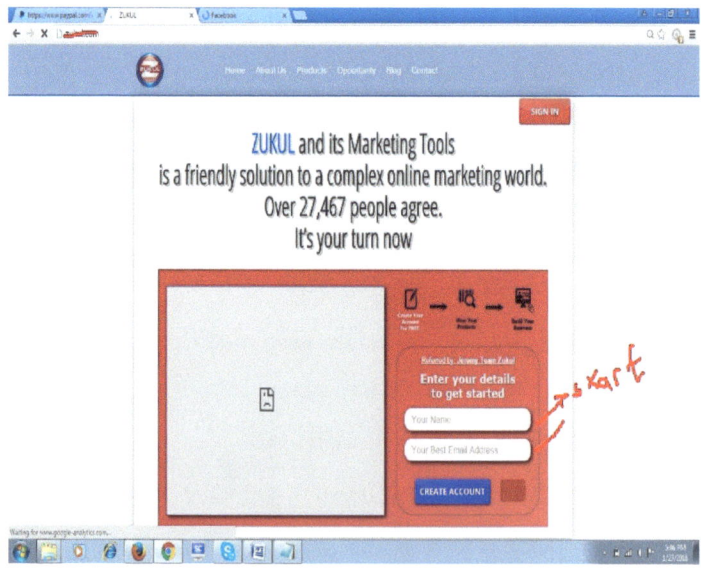

CLICK HERE TO START

INTERNET SUCCESS KEY   *by Yekini Monsuru Abisoye*
How I suffered and how I conquered

Well if you do not want to make an investment in this program, just face the first program I introduced to you alone but to be sincere, you are missing out a lot.

Another way of earning money on zukul is through affiliate program on the platform, and also zukul has numerous marketing tools you can use to build your personal business. I recommend you to read the courses section.

Also you can connect your zukul account with your first ad pack MPA program to maximize your profit.

I guaranty you with this program that your account is going to explode in the next month.

SETTING YOUR ACCOUNT UP ON ZUKUL

Setting your account up on Zukul is easy, go TO MY ACCOUNT on the top tab menu and click on MY PROFILE, put in your necessary information and then click on save.

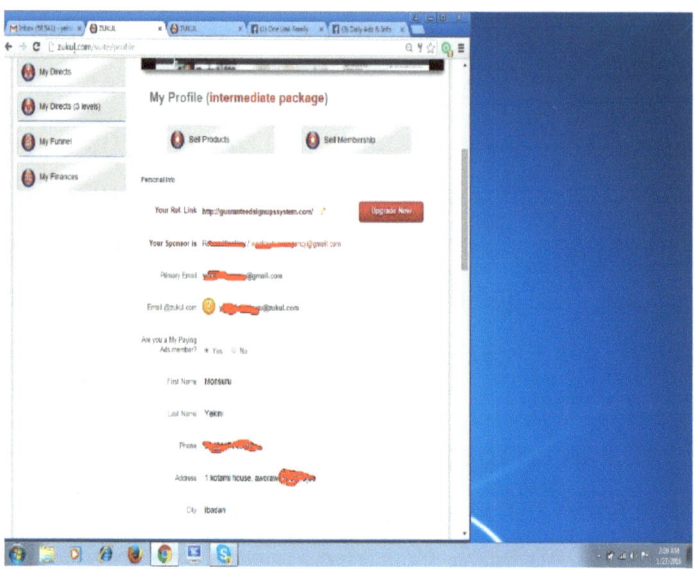

After that, go on to MY COURSES on the top horizontal tab section and make a click on OPENED COURSES TAB, start your courses by clicking on a round red icon, try and view the video step by step. Do not forget while viewing the video, open zukul in another tab, go to my tools and start doing what you are asked to do on the video and before 2 weeks, you will become a powerful marketer and a great income earner.

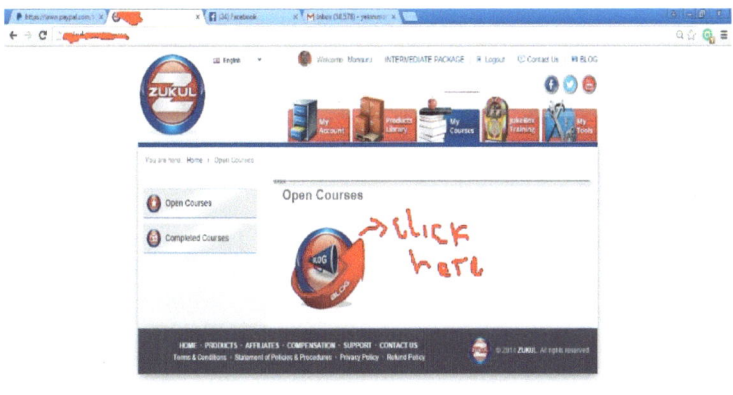

While you are taking the courses, head over to your Face-book account and search for ONE LINK FAMILY, join the group and you will be exposed to things that you have never heard of in online marketing world.

The Skype room is also a fantastic marketing arena; Zukul admin will invite you when it's time, just try and read every email they send to you in your email inbox to move faster.

If you have any question or issue, kindly contact me.

Face book: www.facebook.com/yekini.monsuru

Email: yekinimonsuru@zukul.com

Skype: yatuem.oxygen

I am already been zukuled, will you too?

8.   GUARANTEED SIGN UP

Zukul has been for a long time as far back as 2014 but GSU is new born baby of zukul.

Zukul harbors a lot of marketing materials enough to make an online marketers advertise and make sales online but it was a pity that many failed to understand the power of this great tool.

So there is a need to make people understand the usefulness of this powerful tool and that brought GSU into being.

So experts bring the main sign ups to your business by them and then your business will start growing and growing by itself after the main sign up. So if you like you can use these tools to do more business for yourself and also gain more profit.

The guaranteed sign up is what will call GSU ad pack. You can buy as much GSU ad pack you like to build your business, the more you buy the more exposed your business is, however you can first wait and see result in the first month before buying more ad pack.

To buy more ad pack, click on MY ACCOUNT TAB on the upper horizontal menu and then click FINANCE on the vertical menu, you will then see buy GSU pack, each pack is 3 guaranteed sign up and you will have what will call funnel in which you will earn from till the day of your last breath. Another person you refer will refer and on and on till level 12th in which the income is about $56,900 a month

To be sincere with you, I have not got up to that stage, but I am praying I should and I will be God grace, can you shout a big amen?

THE TRUTH

Every program has is pros and cons, but they   always hide it from people because they are scared that if they know the truth, they will run away and never join.

Now let me use my story as an example, I joined GSU first before joining zukul which cost me $49 and that was for my first 3 guaranteed sign ups which will grow my funnel automatically to the 12th level.

So the next step is to join the main head which is zukul. So I headed to zukul and I joined.

I was told to just do 2% daily of the job by liking their post, commenting and sharing on Face-book everyday whenever I am less busy, that was a piece of cake right? So I do that every day, it even became my habit.

Going to the 10th day, I did not see any sign up, so I was pissed off and headed to the one link family Face-book page to yell at them (you will be on the family page when you join too) and on getting their I spit out what is on my mind and they refer me to their Skype group (my Skype ID yatuem.oxygen in case you want to chat with me), I joined the group and I explained to them what I am going through and before I know it, 2-3 people made a video call with me showing their proof of earnings life, I got relieved a little bit but not totally.

So I asked question further and they explained that GSU work in a rotating manner and that the day I joined and set-up my account, I have been added to the rotator automatically and I saw something like that too, and that I have to be patient more that the sign up will soon reflect. They also said that apart from the GSU pack I bought, my sponsor spillover is still coming directly into my funnel to add more to my earnings.

So I waited for good 3 weeks though before I saw sign up, and after then I started making cool cash from zukul.

The truth is that they should have been telling new comers that the sign up is not immediate rather than letting people in before they gave out the whole story.

But the important point is that they are paying.

HOW THE FUNNEL LOOK LIKE

The funnel start with you, and when you have your 3 GSU delivered or spillover from your sponsor, you will move to the next level, in the next level 9 people will be under you and the after that level is completed, on the third level another 36 will be under you and on and on, you will be earning more money as your funnel grows up to the 12th level.

FUNNEL

YOU

3 people –-- 1st level

(First 3 people will be gotten for you by GSU)

9 people---- 2nd level

27 people-----3rd level

81 people-------4th level

243 people--------5th level

729 people-----------6th level

2,187 people-----------7th level

6,561 people-----------8th level

19,683 people------------9th level

59,049 people---------------10th level

177,147 people--------------12th level

531,441 people----------------12th level

So what do you need again to make money online?

ZUKUL IS THE ANSWER AND KEY TO SUCCESS

If you have any question or issue, kindly contact me on:

Face book: www.facebook.com/yekini.monsuru

Email: yekinimonsuru@zukul.com

Blog: y2mread.zukul.info

Skype: yatuem.oxygen

9. MAXIMIZING YOUR PROFIT

Now, it is high time to teach you on how to earn additional income on MPA and GSU, It so simple and easy. Register with a Safe list, and an example is herculist.com or you can buy targeted traffic from trafficboss.com to your ad revenue program. You can also make a YouTube video indicating proof of your earnings, I am using herculist.com and it has been working for me. You can also buy solo ad from smartlist.com and adhitz.com or even Google ads if you have the money.

Advertise your ad revenue program through your affiliate link, and then people will start joining your team as a free member.

Well free member doesn't add any value to your money on the program, they were there to just test whether the program is working or not, be ready to help, show them proof and convert them, simple as ABC.

Oh I can hear you say easier say than getting it done, well I will tell you how easier it is now and I am sure you will agree with me.

When a free member join your business, go to your account menu and click on referral, then you will see list of your paid members and free members, hit the free members tab and you will see all their names.

Okay roll up the sleeve of your shirt, sit properly and let us find them one by one.

Login into your Face-book account and go to the search menu, copy a member name and search for him/her, add him/her as friend and send a message along with it, I quoted *"Hi, my name is Abisoye, I am your sponsor on MPA. I am ready to help and show you on to make money from it personally, I have real proof that the program is working, let us chat when you are less busy, Thanks".*

Won't you add me if I send you this type of message? Of course you will, after chatting with your free member, show him/her proof of your earnings and I am telling you, if you do this with 10 members, you will convert 7.

The good news is that, once they start buying ad pack, you will have your affiliate share earnings from the pack, as you can see, you are reaping the fruit of your labor.

10.   CONCLUSION

You have your success key on how to make money now on the internet and what you have to do is to open the door to your endless active and passive income for life. Do not hesitate, do not procrastinate, I have provided you with your registration link and how to start.

I know fingers are not equal, if you are the type that doesn't has much money, register with the first program, but if you have a little start up capital, I strongly recommend you to join the two programs. Join the first MPA program in the beginning of this book and then the second program.

The two programs also link to each other in which you can maximise your earnings and make more money.

I am happy you bought this book because your life is about to change for good and I congratulate you for making it a success.

Thanks,

Yekini Monsuru A
www.y2mread.com
www.facebook.com/yekini.monsuru
www.amazon.com/author/y2mread
Skype: yatuem.oxygen
admin@y2mread.com

www.ingramcontent.com/pod-product-compliance
Lightning Source LLC
Chambersburg PA
CBHW041614180526
45159CB00002BC/848